i

c

o

p

e

The #RECURRENT Novel Series is an imprint of
Civil Coping Mechanisms.

For more information, find CCM at:

http://copingmechanisms.net

How To Keep You Alive

BY ELLA LONGPRE

For my brother

I kept myself alive
– Tehching Hsieh

When I was young my Mother told me stories. Walking into the garage, the still hot metal of the gun in what had been his mouth, over his body She heard an echo She said proved god. She encountered his body when She came home, when I was born She gave me his name. She showed me bright orange and blue bottles hidden from her new husband in a drawer, butterflies dissolving into linen.

When I reach our block something is immediately different, though I never see him hanging from the tree. On my way home I miss his body because I take another route that day. That night I begin dreaming alternatives: different slopes that allow me a glimpse of him, suspended from the tree, one last chance at his presence or his voice that would prove something, for me. But from then on I avoid the tree. I redraw my route. My path is always a hyperbola that approaches the edge of the tree but does not meet it. Blocked by my Mother's reflection, a reflection of another possible approach, glimmering.

I try to take a position, but when I lose his body, what does my body relate to. Will I impress other bodies. I have to push aside a branch to see the absence more clearly: the space he once inhabited, what he left contained in it. A ravine: stillness in the earth as it anticipates the return of the stream. A tree, waiting to be tipped on its side, to levitate over the current. I sit on a bench late in the day, watching the face next to me obscure slowly. The last moment I can make out his eyes.

When was the last time you dug. Your body is
the site of multiple digs. How many eras have
passed, or is there a rogue bulldozer, a frantic
re-building. Your body is the site of multiple
digs, civilization-tiered crust.

And what signifies an era in terms of your
body. How and where do the strata present.

Is it helpful to envision the past embedded in
this way, like heaven is above the sky.

Propelling my voice outward, shoeless, then, the world retracts. Outside of the house the ground becomes yellow and the sky, as if he were ascending from the yard. Smoke, rising from the stone building. Two lines of smoke, a helix collapsing. A hyperbola, now. An arc, skirting away. Now the arc is collapsing. It echoes, it's concentric. Why does his absence suddenly inspire a destruction, lighting a circular path on fire. He is buried in the stone. In the tub, ash, mingled with mold edging the caulk: I can't get the smell out of my hair. Soaked with smoke I dunk myself again and again, leaving an impression of myself in the water each time. My submerged body, shimmering, bisected by the surface of the water, half of me is paler, swollen at an angle: containing two lesions, inhabiting two worlds. The one with the lesion that matches mine, I listen to see if she's moving.

Are these even my memories. Memories haunted by my own ghosts and the ghosts of another history: each instance a saga, every site a reiteration, when I lose him does that mean I am becoming Her. The rooms in this house populated with a suggestion, each movement, each sound refines the hint. An eruption: a glimpse of loose tile in the bathroom, suddenly the room contains the narrative. Histories imprint on my body, my density, my frame. My inheritance told to me via language but the unspoken stories passed down body to body. How Her movements trained me to be careful. How often I re-visited a garage I've never been to. How much information can be stored in my blood, my pores, the bone, before it spills. Shaking in the unavoidable humility of my smallness, in the lukewarm water, unstopping the drain but staying in as it empties, so my blood falls with the water level. My blood, dropping.

What are the responsibilities of your body.
How do you forgive your body. What are the
responsibilities of a poet. How do you forgive
a poet. How do you even find forgiveness to
be useful.

How might your skin change. Why don't the
remains repulse you / do you ever let go. What
is *mine*. How do you set aside time for your
body to fall apart. What does it mean for a
body to fall apart.

Trained by the body of another lover left on the couch, empty bottles floating in the spectral water of the room, I found her body when I came home. A dream, at once a prophecy and the adaptation of a myth: a girl, jumping from redwoods; I am sitting at a desk in the forest, bleeding, watching her fall. A matte film now falling on the meadows. Was the dream a prophecy or did I simply ignore the shadows on her face. The dream a shadow I did not utter. Fulfillment of a prophecy: is this a re-enactment? or a new shoot coming up through the trunk of a dead tree.

A new dream now, rows of photographs: the Mother, or me. Eyes painted black against a white sheet. A ball rolls from column to column, drawing a progression, then falls off. How is there music in my mouth now. His words a ball dropped from my tongue and lifting, a smooth glass ball that shows my face, translucent, and my future, another life. In another life I would be on the floor. Singing, but unknown words, but still a song that's known to me, the shape of something brittle. A ball on the water that's also hovering above. When I wake, my body is a diagram, swollen in the places he touched.

Over the grid of the train tracks, the tree's shadow fills in the columns with data, plotting points for potential growth on parallel axes, values fluxing as leaves shift in the wind. The demarcation drawn, rigid, a portal: train, garage, tub, bridge, cracks in the thin membrane between worlds. This is the door he stepped through, and I check to see if he left it open. A matte film now falling on the meadows. Returning to see the tree bow: to him, or, mimicking, or, under the weight. The head of the tree bent toward the power lines, thin arms hailing the sky.

Speak to *escape*.

The State Hospital on the Hill, ruined.

Ruin as a positive change. Not positive in an evaluative way, as in beneficial. But as in: growth. Or increase.

I am with her at the doorway. The girl from the redwoods. White room, white walls. Light in early morning coming through a west window. No: the windows, dark— the buzzing tubes on the ceiling are lit. Cool, translucent cast, giving objects a holy edge. Differing from the white grey of a room at sunrise, walls coated with a skin of milk, glowing from the floor. But the sky is a mirrored ceiling, so everything white is glaring, and close. Milk skin spreading.

This is where I start to distinguish myself— from her—in the doorway. I love her, and this is not my room. Two sets of blue eyes entreating each other, outside the white room. Two needs. The space between us confused by the shapes of these needs, no longer fitting each other. Gently cupping each other. Crowding each other. She needs to take me inside, and I need there now to be a clearly defined space between our bodies. To be no longer doubles on an edge where past steps into present and disrupts the current plane. Gripping any space around me tightly with timid movements to keep more past from slipping through. Or my body.

When I found her. Poured water over her head. Shook her. When she didn't move, bent my ear to her mouth. Hoping the proximity would generate a reverberation. A current of sound beneath my ear, waiting for her mouth to begin exhaling again some sound. I was reverberating.

A flood growing up a wall. Filling a room.

A fire, dying when something has covered it, for instance, a blanket.

Ruin is the blanket.

Filling up a space so there's no room for the voice.

Silence is not empty.

Now she's breathing. In this room. And asks me to come inside. The white walls, high ceiling. Iron grate over the windows. A blank screen, waiting for a projection. A bed screwed to the floor, in the middle of the room, to the scuffed tile. An altar, stifling the room.

On my desk, a pile of old photographs:
the Hospital on the Hill, decaying, fifteen
buildings I used to walk through in college.
Balconies screened by iron grates. Windows
barred. A tree crowding the corner of the
photograph. Climbing the building. Trees
can look like fire.

A tree can look like fire. Housed in glass, a
flame under a hood, a lantern. A large foyer,
round, with a high ceiling. A glass cylinder
standing in the center, piercing the room.
Cutting a hole through it. Reaching from
the floor, opening to the sky. In the glass
cylinder: a tree. Like fire, catching the
light, midday, a wick lighting the foyer,
lamp-light reaching to brush the curved
walls. The floor of the cylinder, hiding the
roots of the tree: stained glass. Alternating
shades of blue indicating water. To cool the
threat of the tree on fire. Values canceling
each other so the cylinder is neither hot
nor cold. Just a light.

A melt. Where green appears. This room waits for a melt. Superimposing the tree cylinder from the foyer onto this white room, hoping to erase the bed. Introducing fire into the milk ice space. So incubation breaks, even for a day. Teeth on the overhang, dripping. But the bed at the center, inhibiting the free movement of fire. A solid mass blocking any possible void.

I am with her at the doorway. And the
nurse, behind. Is there room for both of us.
In the room. She continually threw herself
from a tree, in the dream. While I bled on
the ground. The double continually took
her milk, and drank from it, in the dream.
While the double sat behind me. Is there
room for both of us. After a fixed amount of
time I have to leave the room. But whatever
space my body cut into—in the air—while
I stood –over her on the bed—and was cast
in a shade—

persists.

Standing outside of the room, then.
Outside: my body. Lamb's blood on a door.

The screws that hold the bed to the floor.
One of them is missing. So the bed shakes
when the door closes. Green copper in the
photograph, too. Ruining on the hospital.

Always confused for each other. Are we sisters. Lovers. Later, she remembers only my mouth, her abdomen. Sometimes my tears, her lap. She was not present for the reverberations between my ear, her mouth, listening for a breath. What she was telling me then. A dim flame, coaxing the fire to spread up (the tree). Responsible now for her breath. In an ambulance. Charcoal into her open mouth. Later she remembers me only outside the room.

Out the window. Doing the dishes, what are they doing. My Mother ran outside to stop the new neighbor chopping down the lilac bush, green in late summer with no tell tale purple flowers. Once glowing purple, wild on the side of an empty trailer, swelling the air heavy, buzz and musk, now blank green, wax, nameless bush unrecognizable. Thin branches torn, opening green and white flesh hanging in threads. Wax leaves limp on the grass. Limbs on the grass. Gas powered saw parting lips of bark. A mouth cut into the trunk: jaw unhinged. The bush interrupted to the ground. Limbs blanched by afternoon. Littering the space around the bed, spotting the white room.

On the floor of a blacksmith's during a lightning storm. Steel, iron, stacked on the floor, hung from the ceiling; agricultural tools, gardening tools, affixed to the wall. Watching out the window. The tree on the lawn is struck, by a cord, a gold cord, running to the ground. A limb falling. But only after the metal in the room catches the light. The room flashes, a glow. Then, the crack as the sky is broken and the limb of the tree is snapped.

Ancient oracular practices: carving a question into the scapula of an ox. Ruining the bone with a question. Then throwing it in the fire. What can be revealed by the simple act of fragmenting a body, setting a fire.

Lesions, in the brain, that appear as white flames when a light is shone through. If I'd been born somewhere else I could have been an oracle. Falling to the floor, in a church – body failing the ruin of the brain – appearing to be possessed by a demon, mouth a moaning o – exorcised, as an old man waves a white cotton handkerchief over me. If I remained on the floor I would be a demon.

Water quenches a demon on fire. Cooling the body below its saturation point. Baptized many times, my first memory is of drowning. Toes seeking the scrape of the floor, fail. A bob. Somehow body knowing not to cry out, mouth a silent *o*. Inhaling the world above in anticipation of the succeeding dip below. My brother pulled me out of the water.

Is the design of any structure informed by
the deferral of ruin? White matter –lesion,
or –hyperintensitiy (hole), is the opposite of
a tumor (growth). But when it appears it can
have the same effect on the body. Growth
having the same effect as ruin.

Standing with him on the gulf coast. White sand, a reunion. He denies my drowning. I am incompleted by lesions, he is incompleted by an infection: when his body reached its threshold, they had to take his leg. When he stands in the waves the gulf takes its place. The horizon behind now belongs to his body, and all visual planes behind, collapsed. Unable to pay for a prosthesis, and I am unable to pay for medication. He is living in a trailer where the walls don't meet the ceiling, during hurricane season, sleeping on an air mattress with a hole so each night he sinks to the floor slowly. We have removed ourselves spatially, geographically, still, we have both returned to the place we left.

Though our bodies now have been engulfed.

So there are surfaces of the past we can't cover.

Even as an oracle we would fail to see the drowning. Buoyed by the limb fallen from the tree, the demon survives baptism. My brother's trailer is near a stables. I mow the grass and he uses a chair as a prop at the stove. He takes less at dinner so his son doesn't go hungry. His son washes the dishes, and falls on the porch. At the hospital, a woman who tries tearing off her own skin. I can only bring her water. The stitches now holding the skin beneath his eye.

Throwing into the fire. The hole. What would we eradicate? White cotton, floating.

You can never return because ruin.

Something about this new life makes it harder to dream. Or a dream is happening.

How we look at a world can be a dream collapsed onto another dream. Waiting for a symbol to occur, for an object to acquire meaning and become a symbol that tells you how you are going to continue, or where the passage will be. A hallway lit with memory.

A concept is a memory made hard to feel. An idea with empathy removed. Dying but from across the room, so you don't rub against it, so you don't get it in your eyes.

Ruin is a concept in action. Terrifying because we know to expect it but it is an animal, living, everything it does is a surprise.

Walking into memory, the demonstration of time as a mentor. To be wild but appear ordered.

The shape of discarded lives, relationships, filling my body, determining the shape of how I move. Motion is a gesture into the future, expanding *what you've left* into *what you're entering.* I forgot he had a nickname. This younger church camp minister boy. His shape sometimes determining the shape of my body // his hand // of my hand. Looking for videos of gospel songs, late at night, that we used to sing in dingy lakeside sanctuaries, finding him on YouTube, on the screen, he died two years earlier. I thought he was still at the lake. Still he is on the screen, in the lake. Still I am in the lake. Still his hand // my hand. His voice belonged to my family of sounds. I can mediate distance with technology, I can mediate distance with the technology of language, instead mediate distance with a body. My hand without his hand, suspended, imitating what I remember of the shape. A sign, pointing to division. A video of his wife speaking in tongues, a hand on his casket, sinking. Do we lose control of our bodies when speech can't fill the space created by absence. I know no one who knew him. I find another video, he is speaking. His nickname in the comments section. He is preaching about those who've left God, the chosen path, behind. The screen is telling me in part our story. I watch the video of his wife again. In bed, she is on my lap. I watch her, I find another video, in this one she is singing. I used to know this song. Remembering the words, I fill my house with it. Her voice is in my house. His voice is in my house. In my bed. What do we try to control when there is no space for speech. Again she speaks in tongues, I try to identify a pattern. Her body is using a language that contains what the eulogy hasn't said: how she has lost him. I listen again to her tongues. What does repetition control, when does it become a ritual. Now that I am singing.

What does it mean to lose a body you've already lost: a house you left, eroding. How long has the absence been here, changing the shape of the house.

Or is it only a separation that maintains the integrity of the structure.

What does the return interrupt, the erosion or the house. If there is a return. What is absolved.

To remember it was ten years ago I look up his name on the computer.

A bracelet he gave me, one of the turquoise stones, fallen out.

What are you failing to say. If you are speaking
to someone is one of you still (already) gone /
or is there a delay.

What rituals are useful to locating someone
who's gone.

There is a recurring dream where I live in a new house but there is one room I do not know about, or cannot enter. The house is different each time.

When technology announces death. The nurse on the phone repeats, she's gone. This means I've called a few minutes too late.

The shape of a phone call. To escape one place, and because I can't be in the other, I come to rest in the space of the phone call, and having no sanctuary I call the phone call a sacred space. My brain trips over the phone call. Transposing it. Shifting it earlier. It leaves a smear as I drag it across time.

But what I was going to say to her: Our story has no language. Our stories moving together outside the realm of telling, outside the boundary of the tree diagram I constructed with my uncle in a research library. Our story told in an empty bedroom, pulled aside for a ceramic figurine, a box of china, a paste necklace, telling the younger woman the story of a bruise, of a threat, the story contained in rooms not documents, the story disappeared from our bodies.

You are the medium where two voices meet.
You are the medium where two bodies meet.
Can your body, as an apparatus, modify
another body.

When a woman dies. What is lost. Everything she felt she couldn't say. She only keeps objects tied to unsayable events. In the dream I rode with the woman who was my grandmother into the underground cavern lined with old furniture, a rug painted on the floor, and on the hutch in the back corner all the objects passed down by the women in my family. A tarnished brooch, a plastic box of buttons, a prayer book. The men kept deeds to houses and threatened to take the children. A waterfall breaking out of the checkered tile we couldn't touch. I think about the men we've known who've threatened to kill us, we say nothing because think about their careers. In this way even though I will never have a child I feel I will always be a mother. I think of women I've loved, how her husband terrified her. How no one knew till she died, and still, even then, it was only me. I scan photos of them taken during the depression and note how the watercolor meant to bring them alive looks different on the screen. The tree, a shadow of itself. Sometimes even saying a name can feel disrespectful, but I think of her often. The pink of a rose.

Empathy means you understand how the
world moves,
and how it could move against them,
and you don't want to be the world.

Wisdom means you understand sometimes
they are the world.

Touching her hand: a sheet rumpled on a bed, a ripple free-standing that appears to cover a sleeping body but falls when you touch it. Similar to her prayer book: I was made to sit on the floor and rip the pages apart. The madonna on the cover was heresy because we believed in a father god. A book that opens like hands at prayer, there is devotion built into the object of the book as much as subversion is built into the act of opening. Touching her empty hand, a still hand whose touch was alien but shaped in the way she used to pray.

Filling a book: to arrange the litter on the floor in a sequence. A journal, the dignifying of one's eye. How it organizes.

Songs for god with the I in question. A book is what a ghost is trying to say. Does she become the house or does she become the fire. You don't need much to keep a story.

Time poured off into a glass. The juice poured and I wrote it down, to be wild but seen as ordered. I did not expect the drowning, my body is full with holes. Somewhere I was gushing water to them.

I can't think of a time I was not desirable. The meerschaum madonna on a marble stand, her head is covered by her hair, and a veil, and a halo: smash it, she represents a cult of womanhood, witchcraft, she is not a virgin saint she is a goddess, and she could rescue me. We are no longer allowed to leave the trailer park. A woman's body is shameful and must be covered, a woman's body is desirable and must be uncovered. Unveiled, the original apocalypse.

A woman's body is designed to be brought to its knees. A puddle of orange, dressing up the linoleum, chest flattened against the floor, I lick the puddle. Immaculate. Poverty is clean when it aspires.

Years later: suggesting myself via telephone, he will order them to hang it up, I will want to tell them what I have learned, that none of us can speak. Our story has no language. My loss always in communication with your loss.

Escape will recur. They will leave the trailer by the side of the highway while en route to a chicken farm down south.

The last page of the notebook, a scripture
defining death: water absorbed by the ground.
Blue notebook, a hologram butterfly cover.
Won in a county essay contest on fathers
and matter. Syntax informed by nineteenth
century novels, seventeenth century poetry,
the Bible. Imitating Austen in colored gel pens.
The failure of language.

A house wrapped in contact paper. This rag is ten years of dust. Stacking cans of salted pork from the government in the cupboard. Rooms cleaned everyday by noon, someone might want a tour of the trailer.

This poverty distinguishes from the other kind: there are friends' houses where I can't go because bugs, because disease. This poverty insists itself a temporary lapse: it doesn't belong to the other kind, at least not for long. The myth of this lapse, of poverty's limited duration, articulated in our gaze outward, our aspiration to acreage. The weekly expansion / contraction of a savings account. The three piece suits haggled over at Salvation Army. Wheels on a house hidden by sheet metal skirt. The skirt torn, the myth disproven. Disproven by transgenerational inertia: the bitterness, illness, malnutrition, injury accumulated in the body, surfacing later, poking out through decades of second-hand clothes accessorized by education, gauzy at the seams.

They will reverse the trajectory after the farm fails, we will find ourselves behind the counter at a dry cleaners, a smoke shop, a Burger King. Desperation: sliding bills out of a register when no is looking. Paranoia: slowly feeding them back in. Fist slipping into a deep fryer, skin floating in a tub of water, stamped, She will never be able to wear a watch over the pink and white tattooed sleeve.

We wear our poverty and no one is so distinguished by what she wears as a woman, that is, someone who is hunted. I am wrapped in contact paper, I am clean.

A piece of paper, ripped in three. Edges curling,
the back is red. Writing hidden behind red.
Some substances identified only by their
response to heat.

You thought you were like your grandmother,
her collection of madonnas, filling a room.

Often on the edge of escape I stay to protect the smaller bodies that haven't yet been marked. Then something followed me down the hall this morning. The vent in the kitchen, inflating my skirt with warmth, in the hall a demon or some guide compressing the hairs behind my knees, compelling me toward the bathroom.

TV theme songs pulsing, concentric rings emanating through walls to my bed. Incomprehensible drone, a litany of threat. What remains of a song stripped of melody.

Sleeping under the pull out couch, sleeping on the trundle bed, an aerosol can (hairspray) hidden under the pillow. A hammer hidden under the pillow. Brothers sleeping on cushions. In the dream, the Mother has no eyes, I peel her egg shell covering. Morning, shadows moving on the floor. Something follows me down the hall. The locked door at the far end. Reaching the same point, and returning.

A concrete porch that bulges in winter. Peeling stairs. Something that could be a pipe or a bell, emerging from a broken tile. Stones dotted with weeds, cigarette butts. Wires everywhere, bisecting the lawn, delineating trapezoids part aluminum siding part sky. The clearing: I stop here, and wait. A broken light post, taped. Tape peeling. Edge moving, slightly. Trembling.

An empty box of chocolates, left on a bench in the woods. Gold foil crinkled beneath the clear plastic insert, multiple surfaces reflecting sunlight. Dozens of slopes in every square. Each square a story, each story a graph. This graph, having 3 axes, requires 3 rows of data. The data is plotted on the axes. What inhabits the space between the axes. What about the hyperbolas that approach the axes but never meet.

The tree, flayed, smooth white bone, a femur curvature. Brown ridge of bark encasing the bent tree, bowing to the power line. Antlered ancient thing nodding in assent, reluctant. Grass, the arching back of a sculpture. Water I can't see. Sun still on my back but a breeze the shadows portend finally moving my hair. The raven from all sides.

Faint spray swelling to beads. Sheets of thunder imbricating, sliding, eliding. Grinding fists against each other until the fingers just brushing. Next to me the high pitched clapping of a puddle.

But remembering the small bodies I reverse the trajectory.

The women cover my sopping dress that's materializing my body. He will be angry that I lingered so long in close proximity to the road. There is no inverse relationship in this proximity— decreasing the distance between myself and the road does not increase the probability of flight. Although the ratio of lingering swells over time.

His anger, less at the prospect of losing me than at the tendency in my body to ascend. Envying my ascent: His body has been roped down. Writing His body in my body, behind the red and pink, because my absence is inevitable, His place in His past is permanent. If He imprints its shape in the walls of my cavity deep enough, I will conduct Him out. Transmit Him. Carry a thin sheet of Him out though His substance stays behind. The wax paper pulled slowly from a leaf.

How to write the hyperbola. That approaches the axis, approaches zero, never touching. The slope of the hyperbola appears to taper into a straight line, although mathematically we know that is impossible. That straight line is the turning away, the illusion of escaping your past.

I can't think of a time I was not desirable. This is similar to what we do to keep someone alive: entreat, an allure. Seducing His vitality. *You shouldn't wear a nightgown like that around your father. You're beautiful baby*, and changing my outfit. A woman's body, shame. A shirt under a shirt. A skirt nearly revealing my knees, we burn it. Safety in covering. Design my allure appropriate to desire.

Night reaching, distorting perceptions of scale.

A bath, door locked. I linger in the silent water. What have I displaced by entering here.
Humming a song about the christ, screaming.

The voice carries the weight of the body.
What does hope steal—a process meant to
unveil but instead obscuring, wiping a glass
with dingy cloth.
The performance of escape.

Humming a star. One glowing circle, sliding on the surface of the glass, resting. Caught by a thin film between *aware* and *dream*. And held there.

In Revelation, two people die in Israel.

Determining which history will be conducted by my body, what objects I will impress.

Give something fallen to a stranger, mine is a child. Then I am the one to pronounce.

Celestial object, touches ground: alien, becoming terrestrial, becoming common. Drowning a chair, a tornado eliminates all categories. And the woods.

Escape: beyond performance. A ritual. Meekly approach the edge and stop. Hover, waiting for a sign, to be called forward by the unknown that's poised in the silhouette of your potential. You are caught on the edge, unable to fathom the silhouette, humbled.

What do you name yourself / what do you name a page. What do you maintain even when you've lost [control]. Is it speech. What does it mean to "lose it," as in, glossolalia.

Someone tells me I share a name with the superintendent of the old state mental hospital on the hill. I laugh. The hospital is closed down and condemned, a place I go to walk and take pictures, since I was 18, eight years now. This place scares me because I imagine how easily I could have lived there if I lived in an earlier time. The city is razing the buildings. I research the history of this name online – an adopted name, a legal name, there is no blood relation – and learn that my grandfather has died. Years earlier. I'm sitting at work, on Ancestry.com, there is the death certificate.

From the State Hospital, where you took walks, the superintendent
with your name. This green cupola.

Dome's blue eye. I am beneath the window, awash. What could come through the eye. A basin, and I'm clean.

An astroturf grave. When I'm buried I mean baptized. A mark on a papier-mâché headstone. Chewed paper. We all accompany our own demons. A demon interrupts a dream with a dream. I interrupt the water, perform rebirth. A ritual, you hope you are redeemed. Plunging me under, His hand over my mouth, His hand holding my neck. I come up shaking, He is speaking in tongues, I cannot speak, my tongue, shaking. My tongue silence. My tongue moves in a dream. The accent of my tongue the tension in a room. His tongue against my teeth.

In the dream a room opened by a gun. Waiting for the slaughter, floor perforated. Splintering wood. Another body enters the room and the sky opens. Splinters my mouth.

In antiquity, the cupola had
no cap—only an opening—
the oculus—Latin for eye.
Concentric rings stacked
into a dome, a pupil at
the center. An opening. A
window, a lens.

What lies outside the house?
A tree— and concentricity.
But if a house is a series of
absences, then what lies
outside of the house is: what
has been removed from the
house. Discarded cubes—
but also— discarded bodies.

Redemption is regaining.
When a space redeems.

Simultaneously, you are
returned, returning.

A tree is a line, splitting.

A series of concentric rings,
overlapping. Cut, fall into a
helix.

A tree is a helix unraveling at
different moments.

Ruin is a reorganization of
movement.

Licking the astroturf grave in a dream.
Ripping up a book, but specifically
a notebook in progress. Ripping the
prayer book, smashing the meerschaum
madonna. Under water.

Coming up through the eye. A candle at
the center. Alone, in the bathtub. This is
where I alone touch the water. Singing, I
cup the water in my hands. Staining my
skin.

Absorbing the blue tub. He is outside the
door, moving. My tongue in a dream. He
believes: the devil brought Him back to
life. Visited His father while He slept. Jaw
wired shut.

The Mother at the other end of the house. Her skin stained pink, arm plunged into boiling oil. She has no eyes. When She sleeps She closes a hole over the earth with clay, displacing a dry well. The clay leaks, an eye. Once Her arm held me in sleep. Once we slept. Pair instability. Yielding, skin prefigures submission when it moves. Protective sleeve allowing for motion, I am open.

Lilac unknown to me. Grew by a house I never lived in, in a neighborhood in Detroit where lilac bushes now stand in place of houses. Lilacs permeate the negative space of a house, a room. Scent tracing the frames to indicate the site of the loss, the unnamed longing, the abandonment. A reversal, an opening filled.

Metamorphosis not a
progression: just a process.
Such as in: [primordial]
nucleosynthesis, or, pair-
instability supernova. Ruin
a step in that process. But
also as an agent or catalyst,
present throughout. And the
mold that shapes it.

For instance, rust is a sign
typical of deterioration or
ruin. Crumbling or breaking
apart. But rust is oxidation,
a process in which two
elements combine and
transform.

Abandoned buildings
in Detroit, lining
neighborhoods, catching fire.

Our structure without
our intervention would
deteriorate quickly. Which
is characteristic of nature:
that inevitable growth:
deterioration is generation.
Not a prequel to it. But
structures we mark as
decaying are bordered
by something else that is
simultaneously growing.

Decapitation. A body,
a building. Does the
encroachment of ruin
operate similarly on a body.

Impressing my skin with the rug's
silhouette. Against my spine, braid
uneven against the grooves. Stones
sticking to wet skin, hairs, grains of toilet
paper, dinge. On the floor, I am an object
on the floor, dinge, I take on the quality
of air that surrounds and fills: a cast.

Mother lying. In a bed, stained with
scent, permeated. Tracing Her frame.
Tracing my frame. A woman's body is
designed to lie. On the floor.

A dream of a flood, before the flood. Standing on a roof, above the waterline. Factory rooms below filling with water. Slows, then: water level recedes: evaporating. And the mist solidifies, taking on the inverse shape of the skyline, the negative image of the town. Lifting in a solid block, block breaking away from the outlines of the buildings it'd just hugged (bordered). Lifting and slowly moving away, the town inside out, you can't tell the cloud is moving till you turn your head. Helping a father decapitate the dead body of his son. Washed up. In the dream. Because I'd done it before.

He took the second by the hand. He held His son's skull together when he was hit by a truck. An opening. A toddler unwatched. Staples in skin. The stain on His torso, staples, when He was hit by the train, died and was born again. His body, emptied, my body becomes an acceptable site for His.

Primordial nucleosynthesis:
an origin or a step.

Pair-instability supernova:
instead of becoming a black
hole (implosion, attraction,
inescapable) a star partially
collapses. Collapse. Then an
explosion and dispersal.

The first generation,
or *population*, of stars
dispersed to form the
second. Our star is a third.

Each population increases in
metallicity (a complexity of
components in the core—
stars contain no metal).

No first generation stars
remain.

What keeps us from our
potential,
from rusting, or reaching,
from burning out,
from populating a new
space,
from tending to stay in
motion.

Although interruption of
tendency is future. How
else do we differentiate?
That is, grow.

Wisdom develops as you
accumulate worlds no
longer accessible to you.

When a dog opened the skin beneath
another son's eye He beat the dog like He
beat the devil. Not the dog who split my
earlobe, she started digging holes in the
yard in mourning.

You might imagine forgiveness. If I never
see them again they won't age. Lilacs
permeating the line of a skull. I watch
them when She runs outside to stop the
truncation of the bush. A shovel laying in
plastic grass, smudged with clay. White
plastic.

What texts contain your mythologies.

The banished prophet received a vision from a figure holding a book.
The prophet wrote the vision and called his text the Greek word for
uncovering or *revelation: apocalypse.*
Because the vision revealed was catastrophe, over time the word for
uncovering has come to mean *catastrophe.*

What does disaster unveil. If there is another flood.

Ruin is an apocalypse.

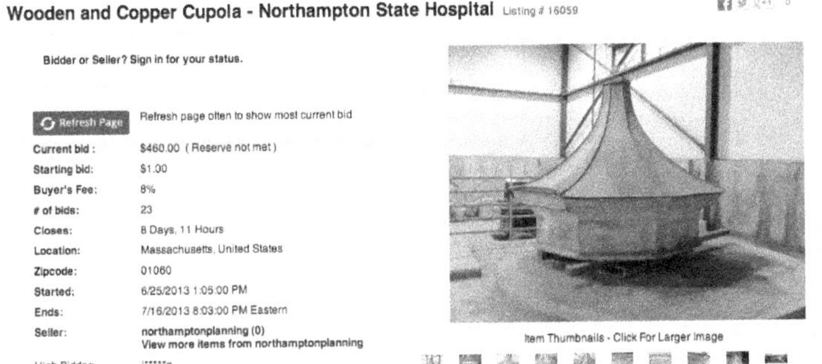

Wooden and Copper Cupola - Northampton State Hospital Listing # 16059

Bidder or Seller? Sign in for your status.

Refresh Page — Refresh page often to show most current bid

Current bid :	$460.00 (Reserve not met)
Starting bid:	$1.00
Buyer's Fee:	8%
# of bids:	23
Closes:	8 Days, 11 Hours
Location:	Massachusetts, United States
Zipcode:	01060
Started:	6/25/2013 1:05:00 PM
Ends:	7/16/2013 8:03:00 PM Eastern
Seller:	northamptonplanning (0) View more items from northamptonplanning
High Bidder:	j*****n

Ask the listing owner a question
Mail this listing to a friend!
Watch this item!

Item Thumbnails - Click For Larger Image

Fifteen buildings, razed. You find the cupola being auctioned off on the internet.

A window is not a mirror, though it at times reflects. A portal that allows you to pass, but on a technicality, and only with great effort. A window confuses two spaces, a point of departure, a prism that refracts beams, the slope of this graph splits open and follows a new trajectory on the other side of the axis, like a tree is a line unraveling. A window is not a doorway you move through, is an eye that lets in light, an oculus at the top of a cupola, looking in, a lens.

A screen is not a window. A screen can appear to be a window or a mirror. A screen protects our eye from the projection of the eye of the image. Looking into the eye of the TV on the shelf bolted high on the wall in the corner of the room. The screen reflects at times, or absorbs at others. In this way it is a window and a mirror. The screen is the portal that refuses to open to you.

A window is something that has been designed to be dismantled. Something that has been closed in order to be opened. Something like the zippered skirt of a girl. This is why we have trouble when the window comes completely undone. Sliding it up and it is suddenly on our shoulder, a window against our body fallen from the wall. A window that leaves its mediating position and joins the room.

On the screen. The last time this TV will play. A lamp, a TV, two glowing points in a dark room. The mirror on the opposite wall that multiplies the points of light so I am hovering somewhere between dim yellow glints and two faces of the same woman who is sleeping with a man and his father, both. Only one of them knows. This is a book I read, wanting to be an adult. Daddy on the TV. When She comes in the window is on the floor and I have given up next to it. According to the open window His car hasn't pulled up yet so She lets herself sink next to me and we, looking down, watch the woman lie to her husband on the window's pale surface. The room is exchanging her image around us, and we are on the floor. For a moment as we bend over the window to lift it and put it back into place, our faces smudge the woman's, or we share a face. When the window is back in its track, She yanks the plug and takes the TV from its shelf, it goes into the shed and gradually disappears or is forgotten. She comes back from the shed but doesn't come back to me, but in a way She does, when She punches the wall in the hallway and this time Her fist goes through a little, and She hovers against the wall like She's levitating until the car pulls up and She goes to her room at the back of the house.

A mirror is not a window, could be a portal or a
doorway but it is a doubling. It is a site of ecstasy,
that doubles us, ghosts us. How we stand outside
our body. A space you already inhabit, a mirror is a
room that goes behind you. And into me. A mirror
is the negative value of the room opposite, points
plotted beneath the x axis of a graph. A hyperbola,
a parabola, a sine curve, the points correspond
as opposites. A mirror adds a negative room to a
room, it voids the room, erasure, how can I make
this room not happen.

She learned to live outside Her body. There was no way She could escape Her body. A silhouette defined by Her wisdom and Her fear, backlight glinting at the edge, She walked attached to it, by a cord. She learned to tie the knot when she was a child. Like many of us. She slipped out, and watched.

Accompanying Her body. When the impressions went too deep, revulsion: its markings, its shape, tugging at the cord. She thought I was her body. Attaching her hand to my arm, dragging me behind, feet cutting a line in the dirt. She thought the house was Her body, and Her fist went through the wall, a hole in the wall the shape of Her hand, an impression on Her body the house had left.

What is the site of ecstasy? Ekstasis: to stand outside. To stand outside our body, to verify autonomy while completely negating it. To inhabit the site of ecstasy disproves the limits of our body. While ensuring we still have a body to return to.

What is the outline of this new site we inhabit, when we stand outside our body. Is this a dream. The soul is extracted from the mouth. Lunar maria, ave maria, a company of horses, a mare and a mare. A horse standing in the sea.

Ecstasy is rage, too. Ecstasy sets in. Like a cast, filling a mold. Once we saw a colorless shape injected with dye. And it began to move. Are we the dye filling a space. Ecstasy means leaving our stain on a room. The nervous system of a house. Even when we ask forgiveness we've left something there.

She wanted to open the house. To step outside. She thought I was Her body, escaping when the impressions went too deep. Interrupting the truncation of the bush. Some warn us we will become salt. Some acts are acceptable out of mercy but not out of rage. To protect lilac and dismantle a house. Was She opening the house for me, too. Then I stepped outside. And She was the body.

When we've left the city and it becomes the dunes. A tree grows from a window on the second floor.

A blank concrete slab, now, that used to hold a house. The house eroding several states away. On the side of the road. Is the hidden story of that house erased. Or dispersed. Bits of paper, caught, floating. The trailer opened.

N
Map
Traffic
Westminster Dr N
Westminster Dr N
Westminster Dr N

Camelot.

The little dog dug holes in the yard, they say she was very sad, that was just her nature. She had eyes like his, especially when the light went out of them. Do you remember? Ours went out at different times, He licked them clean at different times. We were both dragged, I remember that. I keep forgetting: I'm no longer beautiful, I am no longer joyful. I have to work very hard to keep my eyes open now that I have passed to the other side of ruin. A name in a book. White flowers on the table. How to keep ruin from completely growing over you, I have been replaced by ruin, is this even my body I am in. Whose house is this, whose face in the window. If home is tenderness then I once unstrapped a small body from a stretcher and held him to me so that we breathed together until he stopped shaking. I was his apparatus. A lost boy, a small child, they came to find me, hesitant to take responsibility for his body, a lost boy, this was one of the last times I saw him, if you never see them again, they don't age, I have trouble remembering if this is the time the light went out of his eyes. We could not speak in the house. I worship the space where I can still speak, a cylinder with the ends cut off, a cardboard tube you look down. I ask someone, is this the divine. But there is no one. A hand comes down over the end. He's taken the dog out to the shed, we were both dragged, I listen to see if the dog comes back, I know for certain when He comes back too late with dirt on His chest. But before He comes back it becomes obvious after a certain amount of time that the moment has passed.

Cold van, scarf undone. While we wait. We, and the other children, go with Him to shovel the church parking lot. Red sweat pants. The first in the prayer room. Waiting for a pastor to unlock a door. *He was not evil, He had great potential.* A gift to god in the form of a service performed with the knowledge and experience of poverty. Dark prayer room, a scarf undone. A gift to the god with no eyes. Eyes closed, a gift unseen, I mean to fill god's heart. Instead I fill the room. Traces of me still on the wall. Which is god's body again, the room or the bread, I am in him or he is in me.

The sun melts a light around the corner that lifts, a vapor, into our mouths.

A closed door, the white stone wall of a church, boarded windows, in a field I pass on my bicycle. An opening in the back, a slit in a board I peer in, seeing only a space the light doesn't hit. An opening in the wall a small animal has made. The eye of a hollow brick. The pupil is a hole that lets in light, what does it let out. What spills out of the eye.

Ruin animates an abandoned space,
enters a space to keep it current.

Space exists as a function of motion.

When we've ceased to love, and bitterness enters.

Tearing up the page you couldn't finish writing.

Memory like language and sex binds together two unlike things.

Ruin is duration.

Ruin is not a visual characteristic. Ruin is duration. Ruin fills a space while opening it.

A room over time. Who I am.

I become more complex when ruin begins to escalate.

The tradition is to set fire to abandoned buildings. A father and son die. Given another chance they grow old, up, they die again. I watch this second death with Him, on TV. The boy who lit the lighter is a man with his mother, they have a pool now, he looks like a boy in the suit he borrows to wear on TV. We miss school for the father and son once, but the second time the leaves don't even pause their trembling. They live alone in a cornfield I pass on my bicycle after school. They live on the run-down block by the fairgrounds where we drink mushroom tea and watch photo slides projected onto the snow, two slides jammed in the projector at once, so when we adjust the focus one image soaks into the next, a piece of paper falling on a spill.

He is the one who gave me the idea for the fire.

A bone person, someone you see through. They live alone in a cornfield. When he speaks, what is behind him. Standing, heavy with empty. A creek appears in the frozen ground, he is bleeding. A creek appears in the sky. The father and son are caught in a circle, what happens to a circle under water. When we try to put out the fire. Another way to be locked in a room, another way to be lost in a room. *A locked door,* He said, *why didn't they break it down.*

I believe the devil takes different forms: a book, a kindness, the concern of an old friend. A devil can be someone who was taught how to behave. The devil is something that is transmitted. His father told Him the devil stood over His bed and let Him live when He was hit by the train but that was the devil talking. Sometimes when the girl was there we were both dragged, he took the second by the hand. We kept a garden and the children picked the beans and peas and we canned pickles and tomato sauce and later, when we went back, the cucumber vines had grown up the shed wall and the dahlia stems looked like pumpkins curling across the ground. I remember the way he said *pumpkin* and *cock-a-roach*, and I remember looking down at his face, trying to regulate his breathing, his inhuman eyelashes, and by now, he would have been a man.

In the dream I am one of two women. In the kitchen we've locked
the door, but we can see the figure moving past the window.

I had a lover who thought he was an oracle. He dove into a pool
and re-surfaced, no longer breathing. He is always seeking descent,
he is still trying to return. He tried to break in in the middle of the
night, I mean, he called in the middle of the night. He is not the
one who died.

In the dream kitchen, the floor is opened from below by a shotgun.
Then another shotgun comes through the door, opens her mouth,
then mine. The devil is something that is transmitted.

My Mother / I had a lover who tried to break in. My Mother had a
lover, who I had, a lover. I have Her legs. I have a dream that She's
laid out on a white sheet. Her kohl-lined eyes are closed. It is me.

In the dream a black rattlesnake, moving through the creek. I
can't hear it over the water, I can't see it under the water. It jumps,
latches onto my hand. I don't die.

You must believe in the spiritual properties
of objects, otherwise how will these objects
prove powerful to you.

For instance, flower foam, bones, etc. We can
wrap silk, we can bring candles, we can choke,
we can store under the bed, we can take from
the dog.

We can make impressions, we can write our
names.

Solving the riddle of the Sphinx.
There is something beneath the surface you
have to reveal. But whether it's your memory,
or one from the communal pool, or

the apocalypse: brushing away the soil,
holding the bones, what will you do with
them, how do they taste, whose name,

brushing the soil, the epiphany, the revelation,
the erasure, the ruin.

My Mother had a lover, I had a lover, who came to visit me at church camp in summer, the older girls did my hair, She recovered from a miscarriage at home, a yellow blanket on the couch, an empty seed pod. A red jacket from the wrong decade made me a woman from a movie. The lake, He and I walking at night. The lake shone through the cabin in the daylight when all the girls told jokes on beds and shrieked at something the Bible didn't teach us, we were an age where you had to cover your body with yards of fabric but we still had our shining hair. We still snuck to the lake at night and showed it parts of our body the sun wouldn't see.

At a bigger lake, I was younger, before the lover, at the silver lake at night edged by sand dunes. I practiced my witchcraft under the moon and fed the ducks cheese-filled pretzels on a bench by the water, away from the tent, in a nightgown I thought a hippie or a faerie would wear. A photograph, me in a purple bathing suit next to a brother who was gone, knee deep in the water. The photographs are lost in a house I can't access. All memories of a brother, in the water, a hurricane, you'd think he was the one who died.

I hold a film strip of her face against a white sheet.

A legend about the dunes: a bear and her two cubs swim across the water,
escaping a famine. The cubs drown, becoming islands.
The mother lies down on the shore, surrendering, and becomes the dunes.

You could recreate a book of photographs. A line of questioning you don't
anticipate emerges:

how far from memory have you come?

You discover your mother, your lover, has been lying to you. You're not loved in precisely the way you thought you were. And you have to decide whether you walk away.

According to some Algonquin tellings, Glooksap created humans by shooting arrows at an ash-tree: we came crawling out of the gash. The creator wanted a loon for a dog. In tales that originate in different locations around the globe we help the divine cross a river. Sometimes the ruin of a relationship means to draw nearer.

A relationship is a plane separating two people. A length of opaque fabric between them. Or maybe each is wrapped in a cloth envelope. You can't see one another's envelope, you have to trust the voice of the other. Even when you're pressed against each other, touching hands against the cloth.

A dream, at once a prophecy and the adaptation of a myth. A dome, a miniature replica of a blue hemisphere. If someone offers you the sun, don't respond bitter moon. I could weep.

Can you believe a dream that foretells your own death. Dreams, parents, meaning well lie to their children. To help them take in the world slowly and easily, and sometimes shock them with truth necessary to go on. So like with parents it's often unclear whether to trust a dream.

Mellowed lilacs, the bush cut down to the ground, limbs scattered on the lawn. Cradling the limbs in my arms, choking on the blossoms.

Ruin is
not a structure falling but two separate planes, meeting each other.

The soul is extracted from the mouth. The speculum is the bright patch
of plumage on a bird. Sometimes we are revealed in something we didn't
expect to see.

The bird could be a dog, whining.

Nothing is broken.

Ruin is not necessarily a failure.

Something about absenting yourself. I wanted to ask Her, Do you have to leave everything behind. What I don't understand, how / are You distinct from Your body / enough to extract Yourself. And what is the new site of you, are you the room, in moments of ecstasy does the room become your body. Is that why we say a house is haunted. Holding your hand up to the window, hooking your finger into a hole in the screen. If the room is your new body is the window the hole the soul is extracted from. I climb the stairs and the room throws me back. I climb them again and reach the top each time, then fall to the bottom. In an act of forgiveness I stop climbing the stairs. I tried to get to the lake. Is this Your new body, an orange bottle bobbing on the surface. Would You drown me. Would You keep me alive. When you keep someone alive, what is kept alive. You often never returned. When you refer to someone who is still living in the past tense, what have you done. In the dream the Mother has no lips. I am the one who cannot speak. If we could create an opening in our skin, for the unsaid, pull it apart and look through.

I climb the stairs and You throw me back. I climb them again and reach the top and each time, You push me, I fall to the bottom. In an act of forgiveness I stop climbing the stairs.

In an act of forgiveness I stop climbing the stairs. Reconciliation can negate forgiveness: giving You the chance to do it again when You want to become something else. Reconciliation means You are still the one who threw me down the stairs.

Here You appear so I can forgive You. Here You appear so I can be absent.

In an act of forgiveness I give us both the chance for another scenario. In an act of forgiveness I name what You've done, I give it my own name, "I" am now what You have done and I have disappeared.

In an act of forgiveness she excuses herself from the table. You remove the table (throw it against the wall), the table is now what you have done and she has disappeared.

In an act of forgiveness she leaves the room. In an act of forgiveness she takes her child. In an act of forgiveness he is on his knees in tears and you say nothing. In act of forgiveness you tear a page out of the book. In an act of forgiveness you leave your old life behind.

Forgiveness is not always possible. It is indecent. You can't absent yourself, your ghost stays behind. This is what they mean when they say ruin is a haunting. Ruin is transmitted. What is lost is haunted, too, by what stays behind. You are haunted by the house.

A dream can be a space of forgiveness. If you don't leave it you become wild. Forgiveness can be a dangerous movement into the past, and slight. A revision. And when you linger you start slipping back, the woman rolling down but crawling up the hill.

Sometimes it's the other who has to go. Then I becomes you again.

You handled that very well.

The house holds out his hand. Inviting her back in. The house has already begun to fall apart, a trailer left by the side of the road, a small wooden cabinet inside with a mirrored back. This is where the dog ran from room to room in a dream. How to make this room not happen. A small wooden girl with a mirrored back, and you follow her. The small wooden handle of a knife, and you follow her. A small wooden girl at the bottom of the stairs.

I like it when the skin is loose. It comes off in one piece, and then you have an empty world on the table. Some of us are so impressionable we take on the shape of any room we are in. Once in a dark room I kept the house from falling in, someone I loved was outside trying to break through a door. The delicate one with flowers. If he kicked through the glass door how would that affect the body. What portion of the mouth, promising to break a window, unravel the body. I dreamed in glass, the light out in the bathroom and the door locked, dialing numbers with a hand over the screen, it emitted no light, if you keep your house dark always they will see you are afraid. Hitting the middle of a heaven, starless. Making impressions is a form of control, he was used to making impressions on me, taken off guard when I calcified and so when he knocked over the lamp I felt like I could fall over and crash, or the glass door he was kicking. It's not enough to see through a house, a body, you have to break through a house, a body. Is there a science to this, we always hide in the bathroom when someone threatens us with a boot. We didn't recognize control, we thought it was a form of love. Years before on the same day actually a man in the middle of the night, naked, trying to break through a glass door, we lock eyes, is there a science to this. Do they realize your body is the house or is it less menacing, they just want to get to your body. To be strong you don't hide in the bathroom, but what do you do. A stain of black paint on the wall by the tub, is there a memory to this. Will they always expect to leave impressions. How did I find Him again. I would like to be wild in this room I have locked myself in, the island that has fallen apart. Green against grey, everything has grown somehow and each house is hidden by the swollen trees, and now there are islands. He is trying to get in. I try to keep a tree in each room but in this room the tree looks like fire. The tree edging the corners of this room like the blackening edges of a photograph.

If they can't make impressions they expect they can break you.
Like if you are not flux you are rigid. But they forget you are wild,
too, and you can sense the air shift. They cut the lilac bush to the
ground but never dig out the root so the ground starts to sink and
the tiles fall apart. You can sense the air shift and know to move
around it like the tree in this room now is growing up the wall,
that is, it's glowing, a room on fire, if they see your house is dark
always they will not be afraid, you open the blinds so the window
becomes a screen playing the fire, a mirror you watch it on, on
this day, years ago, the man at the door can he see you, too, there
is no way you can let him into this room, in an act of forgiveness,
he wants to become ruin, in an act of protection you are become
ruin, they never expect you to be wild, always something that
depresses or snaps, never something that moves.

I keep trying not to, but I find myself living again and again. Sometimes it seems like the most compassionate act you can perform for the world is to not participate in it. Then part of it falls apart when it loses your support. Is this community. Or narcissism. The audacity of keeping yourself alive.

When he asks why you left.

It wasn't the stretcher, where the light went out in his eyes. It was a thousand times before that. Returning to a scene I thought would have waited, suspended, the atmosphere is the same but important objects have been replaced or removed. Bodies have changed. But there He is, like the boy in the cornfield with his father, tethered together in a house on fire. The Mother has no eyes.

What we understand about death is how people move around it. Ruin is that dance.

It's wrong to let a child die. In the dream the pool of children, face-down. I'm too late, except for one whose eyes are like mine, I take her with me. In a house further up the mountain, they've left me behind and forgotten the newborn calf. I call her ox and she looks up from my lap so her matted hair falls in her eyes and she trusts whatever I might do to her. The child is waking.

At first in the dream the flood came from the bed. I found the key
to the wall where the letters of the dead woman were kept. That
was when the flood started, growing slowly in the house, pouring
from a hole in the middle of the bed like an unseen sea flowed
under the mattress. Later in the dream that spanned several days
the bed was the mouth of the river, in a cave. The river seemed to
come from the ground, I guarded the cave, it's unclear whether
this was the bed I slept in alone or the bed I shared.

Crumpling paper, like dropping dye in water—records movement
and substances we don't otherwise see. In the dream the floor
opens. I think of the practice of foot-washing, humbling yourself
in front of another, a basin, a vessel that waits to be filled as a
service, sometimes that means to receive violence.

A door that opens onto a wall.

There was a family before this, too. Something you learned from
childhood is if we are trained to distrust each other there can be no
uprising. A city that's not supposed to work.

I mean to reorganize the divine.

I am, unfortunately, evil. A demon in a dream, in the hallway, in the corner of the room when I wake. I touch myself when you're not here, afraid you'll find me. I lay in the bed, wrapped in the muslin I'll wear for the pageant, singing about the christ, he's risen. A demon, risen from the floor. It takes the shape of the room around it but fills with dye. Injected with ink. Injecting a space with ink, but isn't that what I'm trying to do now, remembering with a pen, staining the space in the room with ink. Smudging the demon. My evil is a stain you can't help but lap. My evil is a necessity of my body and the space it occupies in you, whatever shape my shape inspires in you, an erect shape, my shape is malleable as my understanding of this room, you could open the window and I would flux, you delight in this flux, the flux of my body makes you more rigid, more distinct, the fact that I bend and fold into the scenery and could be any object makes you hard. The more malleable I become the harder it is not to touch, and the Bible tells us tempered silver is the most pure. The Bible is not interested in the flesh, not like you.

Death followed me down the hall this morning.

Death is just that, is an angel, not a demon. It sits in the correct realm, accompanies without threat. For instance, a demon appears at the window and becomes the glass and the glass will catch you as you move through the lit room and can take you with it. A demon interrupts a dream with a dream. A demon, though underwater, insists on talking to you. Death simply walks with you down a hall.

Attracted to the concept of his own dangerousness, a man I knew spoke often of his acquaintanceship with the devil, who was officially affiliated with death. The devil like death is an angel not a demon. The prophets have washed themselves to receive the story, the devil is the storyteller, he was named after light and his voice is a type of pipe organ. A demon will visit you, he is very polite, wearing a hat he will remove it in the parlor where you lay recovering. A demon is your bridegroom, the devil is the wind at the concert.

I am, unfortunately, evil. I don't understand space outside the room. I enter the outside and expect the demon. But if the demon takes the shape of the room and I am walking out into open sky, what shape is the demon. I expect to be followed by a stain, but the air is clear, somehow, as if I am not evil out here. But I have seen the demon. And I am afraid I've carried it out in me. And its ink fills me, I am the room, now. A body becoming a room when it steps outside. The ground becoming a seat when it is sat upon, the air breath when it is breathed. A demon outside becomes a cloud in my belly, heavy, invisible, a moveable stain.

I am, unfortunately, evil.

To know, not just, you are different, but *how* you are.
There is a charm to it.

A compulsion. An assignment. It is not something one does but a perception. Because I am now outside, it is how I am marked.

The devil is a necessary agent in rebirth. A demon is an agent in redemption. Not always present, sometimes a guide, a sage, a trickster. A demon interrupts a dream with a dream.

> The concept of the demon is in you, you are an agent of your own redemption.

I have come to trust demons, though I used to dream they were always behind me or watched me sleep. A demon followed me down the hall one morning. I ran to the bathroom and locked the door. Waiting for the demon to retreat, I baptized myself in the bathtub.

> Someone may try to correct your definition of the term *demon*, to reconcile it with their own version. But we all accompany our own demons.

Luckily I know I am capable of terrible things.

The Gospel is made up of four books, four different versions of the Christ, a different man hangs on the tree each time.

Forgiveness is not necessary to redemption. That is, those you have hurt may not recognize your new life, they don't ever have to. You are often given a new name upon rebirth, especially when it involves baptism. However sometimes the thing returned to you during redemption is your own name. Can you imagine returning to the world, in your old clothes, as if you are who you used to be.

There is no safe space. Where I come from violence is sometimes necessary. The smell of the air changes in summer as a response of the earth to sustained heat, dirt getting warmer, over time. The Mother wouldn't let us leave the house, to keep us safe.

Over time a house becomes as immense as
conversations with god, begging him to confide in
you because he must be lonely. A house is divine and
alchemical as the sun's light changes you through it.

Leave your old name behind but your love for it will follow you down this new path, protect it, what you smell now is the dirt turning to ice.

Looking at the map on the computer of my old life I can see that the tree is gone. So he is suspended from nothing, he hits the ground. In an act of forgiveness. He could never separate himself from his failure to keep himself alive, he could never forgive himself. Passing the tree every day I could never forgive him. We exchanged looks. Now the tree is gone the rope that tied us to it dropped.

It was a lumberyard, that's where the tree stood, standing on the edge of the yard, over overgrown train tracks. We would cut over the tracks on our way home from town, just over the tracks from the lumberyard was our block, his house was first, with the balcony that looked over the road and sometimes he would call down as I passed his house to get to mine on the corner. I stopped to sit barefoot on a porch on that block smoking a cigarette with a neighbor friend because I didn't want him to call down to me that day, when another neighbor friend called me across the road, and I skipped over like in a playful way toward danger, and she told me that he'd just done it from the tree over the tracks. Essentially I'd just missed him. So for the next year walking home I couldn't avoid him at all, whichever route I took I encountered him. By now the neighbor friend has moved, his room is empty, my house is empty, and from the other side of the country I hear the lumberyard is being turned into a café or a law office, so the tree is gone, and a fence has been put up along the tracks now that the train is running again. And it's like someone has come by and opened up a room my body with a wrecking ball because if grief and memory aren't just as contingent upon space as they are on time.

In an acknowledgment of the contingency of its power fire clings to a log. Rendered impotent it leaves behind ash as an artifact of its movement. The conduit has been changed by the current.

106

Fire can erase the marks of time or, impatient, finish the work time has been too hesitant to do. To you, a tree is a child, to me, a tree is something that does things slowly. Do we attribute all our fears to time.

A relationship doesn't just happen over time, it is a shape drawn on the ground as two figures move in relation to each other. I move away from you, I move toward you; or, I move toward you, I move away from you; the shape of the relationship is the same, either way the same area.

Before or after aura. The shadow of the tree.

Telling the tree, opening and revealing concentricity.

As allure, I write of the electricity of what I write.

Putting up a fence: interrupting a trajectory, dictating a detour, ruining a space by defining it, as with a word. If a tree is a helix unraveling at different points in time, then cutting it down limits how many threads will and where they will extend. It's also erasing a reflection from the surface, which is the ground, and the original image that lies underneath it, like making a ghost. In the dream at the party I escape by going into the basement and look for the boy hanging in the immense blue tree, I know I'll never find him. With a tree cut down everything hanging from it finally gets a chance to lay. A fence takes time to walk around; putting up a fence means you could be several years away from a point you're separated from by only a few feet.

Returning, upon arrival, the morning after the storm, the island seems wild, like everything is on the ground because the island left it there, and swollen. I am a vulture. Some people cry out. The vulture landed in the road in front of the truck and would not move, maybe it was you. Can you imagine if we gave up control. Narrating what happens next, underneath or above, I can't tell.

Ruin is a story happening, obviously. That a building could fall over time. How could we let this happen, the explanation is not catastrophic but mundane and this slow atrocity attracts us. What has to happen to a public for a city to fall apart. What has to happen to a family for a room to fall apart. Sometimes a house is always falling apart before we see it. A crack coming up from under ground.

Truth is a form of self-protection, if we forget the truth, we could be anything. I may or may not be wild, depending. In this room I have made a vow of strength, to cut out potential threats to integrity. But in the quietude of this room I have locked myself in, a small hand opens the space in my chest dedicated to questioning and I feel the vulnerability of a wound trying to close itself, the desperation that I'm working too slowly, or maybe I should refuse to heal, in the manner of evolution become a new opening, because strength and preservation guarantee structural integrity, but vulnerability allows for the potential inherent in chaos, embedded in every error.

You are still alive but the refusal of certain bodies to re-form themselves simply means the world around them will have to adapt. The more we shape the world the less we will become.

The blue falls from the tree in this room, it is gone and
has no name.

I took out the color from Her face. Her iris I was not sure. Because
then the ground got colder. I mean then Her eye was ice. I mean
then Her face was blue dusk, a wet forest behind. How many
moons are in the window, now I'm under water.

We all have apocryphal texts. What we can't let out, an effort to
make ourselves. Holes like angels.

To die, as a child, and continue (living).

Why are the crows in the stream. A globe in the water. Purple
jungle gym.

The mirror is an act of ruin.

A mirror beneath an oculus, at an angle. Serving as a lamp. An eye is a light.

The speculum appears in a dream. Cool metal wall at the end of a long tunnel, reflecting the distant mouth: a speck. Disintegrating a mirror, the only way to destroy a reflection. Speculum mundi, the act of holding a mirror up to the world.

Ars moriendi, fifteenth century book on: how to die. The art of dying, the joy of dying gracefully. Illustrated.

An index of fifteenth century English woodcuts, in a library. No illustrations. Four hundred pages of one-line descriptions.

Far left: a tree. Left: a demon. Right: a woman holding a mirror. Far right: a grid on fire.

You will always return because ruin. An ocean, a collection of summer. Which population of star. A collapse and dispersal we barely see, an oracle can mean a place, an oracle can mean a prophecy, an oracle can mean a girl. How do you fulfill. An oracle disregards time's structure but acknowledges its passage. Like someone speaking to you. A hand on the bed getting lighter.

Setting this room on fire. My Mother's stories, lighting the book.

To some extent the fire will take care of itself. There's enough you wish you hadn't done. The tree on the edge of the room, in the corner where two pressures meet. In the corner where the ceiling waits it becomes clear the room is doing something, holding itself up for the sake of what's inside against whatever is about to fall. I sleep closer to the wall, it can fold over me if it needs. Holding itself apart until time lets the air out. When you feel unsettled in the hall in the morning like something is behind you it's not just the history the house holds but the time that hasn't leaked out yet, everything that is going to happen, the size of the fire lets you know how much time you have left.

Ruin is a prayer I say at the end of love. To create an index of the images meant to guide you through death. If there is some indication there of which angel is to bring you, or offer you a wooden box with a book inside, how would you get yourself ready to receive her. Collect the implements listed in the index. Recite.

There are several maria. Aside from the virgin there are seas on the moon. Lunar surface reflecting light at different intensities. Over a field, a company of horses. They came to meet me at the fence on walks at night when I was in the meadows, far from home. And then a prayer on a bead or at the foot of a stone. A crown of light to melt the stone. A gift of stone to a young girl. I am an icon. A wall opens to collapse two planes. Within the frame, so I can fall out not through. I am offered a key but the opening. Morning approaching. Surrounded by maria, an incantation, there is one of me.

The cosmology revises itself. A small world. An offering. You are absent. At night a sundial is all time, which is why the world is unmoving. A grey net, dropped, catches at the edge, tears at the slightest movement. An array. Only a handful of these bodies are present. A crown, dropped. This room is spectral water, a body must have volume to displace. What does it mean for a volume to be an inverse: a vacuum. You not here the room is lighter. I feel I am going to fail.

Death followed me down the hall this morning. Now you have no reflection. And as the sky shifts pink to accommodate the day, I make a hole for a small soul in my throat. Christ has returned to the passion, we are both on the edge of vacuum.

Ruin as the growing of negative space. The space of time. Fire a way to keep ruin from happening, or to happen quickly. As the book is ripped apart someone's hand moves over it.

You don't need to know his name. The Bible is not interested in the flesh. What the man with the Bible was telling me was that we'd both ripped apart holy books. What I mean is we'd both torn apart something sacred to us. In order to keep you alive. I could live in a place where I have a mother.

II Samuel 14:14

for we must needs die, and are
as water spilt on the ground, which
cannot be gathered up again.

Acknowledgments

Many thanks to Bhanu Kapil for suggesting I break my writing open. Thanks to J'Lyn Chapman for watching over the development of this book. To JH Phrydas for reading it. To Vanessa Hersey, Jaclyn Hawkins, Ben Hersey, Katie Dyer, and Indigo Weller for conversations that informed it. To Sara Veglahn, Renee Gladman, Tracie Morris, Melissa Buzzeo, and Ariana Reines for reading drafts and excerpts. To Anne Waldman, for her support.

Excerpts of this book have appeared, in earlier forms, in *Lunamopolis, A Bad Penny Review,* and an untitled chapbook published by Awst Press.

OFFICIAL
CCM ◑

GET OUT OF JAIL
* VOUCHER *

- -

Tear this out.
Skip that social event.
It's okay.
You don't have to go if you don't want to. Pick up
the book you just bought. Open to the first page.
You'll thank us by the third paragraph.

If friends ask why you were a no-show, show them
this voucher.
You'll be fine.

- - - - - - - - - - - - - - - - - -

We're coping.

◑

CPSIA information can be obtained
at www.ICGtesting.com
Printed in the USA
FSHW020951080819
60843FS